NUREG-1745

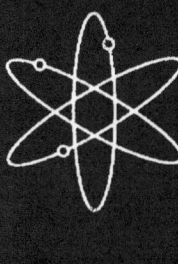

Standard Format and Content for Technical Specifications for 10 CFR Part 72 Cask Certificates of Compliance

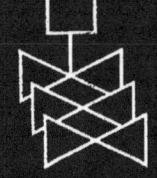

U.S. Nuclear Regulatory Commission
Office of Nuclear Material Safety and Safeguards
Washington, DC 20555-0001

AVAILABILITY OF REFERENCE MATERIALS
IN NRC PUBLICATIONS

Standard Format and Content for Technical Specifications for 10 CFR Part 72 Cask Certificates of Compliance

Manuscript Completed: May 2001
Date Published: June 2001

Spent Fuel Project Office
Office of Nuclear Material Safety and Safeguards
U.S. Nuclear Regulatory Commission
Washington, DC 20555-0001

ABSTRACT

The Standard Technical Specifications (STS) for dry cask storage are intended to be used by potential 10 CFR Part 72 Certificate Holders in developing a set of clear and consistent technical specifications for their dry cask storage applications.

The NRC believes that these Dry Cask STS in this NUREG will assure the overall safety goals for dry cask storage are met, including maintaining subcriticality, controlling radiation dose to the workers and the public, assuring fuel retrievability, and maintaining the confinement barriers. This effort has removed the unnecessary detail from the technical specifications, moved the less significant requirements to administrative programs, made the requirements less prescriptive and maintained consistency with the site specific requirements contained in 10 CFR 72.44. Although these STS were developed for Certificate Holders, the format and level of detail presented in this set of STS can easily be translated to technical specifications for site-specific licensees.

PAPERWORK REDUCTION ACT STATEMENT

The information collections contained in this NUREG are covered by the requirements of 10 CFR Parts 50, 72 and 73, which were approved by the Office of Management and Budget, approval numbers 3150-0011, 3150-0132 and 3150-0002.

PUBLIC PROTECTION NOTIFICATION

If a means used to impose an information collection does not display a currently valid OMB control number, the NRC may not conduct or sponsor, and a person is not required to respond to, the information collection.

TABLE OF CONTENTS

ACKNOWLEDGMENT

The authors wish to acknowledge the valuable contribution of the members of the Standard Technical Specification Task Force consisting of Christopher Bajwa, Kenneth Erwin, Adelaide Giantelli, James Randall Hall, Geoffrey Hornseth, Henry Lee, Chester Poslusny, and Bernard White, IV. Without their significant contribution and support this document would not have been possible.

NRC FORM 651
(3-1999)
10 CFR 72

U.S. NUCLEAR REGULATORY COMMISSION

**CERTIFICATE OF COMPLIANCE
FOR SPENT FUEL STORAGE CASKS**

Page   1   of   4

The U.S. Nuclear Regulatory Commission is issuing this Certificate of Compliance pursuant to Title 10 of the Code of Federal Regulations, Part 72, "Licensing Requirements for Independent Storage of Spent Nuclear Fuel and High-Level Radioactive Waste" (10 CFR Part 72). This certificate is issued in accordance with 10 CFR 72.238, certifying that the storage design and contents described below meet the applicable safety standards set forth in 10 CFR Part 72, Subpart L, and on the basis of the Final Safety Analysis Report (FSAR) of the cask design. This certificate is conditional upon fulfilling the requirements of 10 CFR Part 72, as applicable, and the conditions specified below.

Certificate No.	Effective Date	Expiration Date	Docket Number	Amendment No.	Amendment Date	Package Identification No.
XXXX	XX/XX/XX	XX/XX/XX	72-XXXX	0		USA/72-XXXX

Issued To: (Name/Address)

Safety Analysis Report Title

CONDITIONS

This certificate is conditioned upon fulfilling the requirements of 10 CFR Part 72, as applicable, the attached Appendix (Technical Specifications), and the conditions specified below:

1. CASK

    a. Model No. XXXXX Cask System

    The XXXXX Cask System (the cask) consists of the following components: (1) a canister which contains the fuel; (2) a storage overpack (XXXXXX), which contains the canister during storage; and (3) a transfer cask (YYYYYY), which contains the canister during loading, unloading, and transfer operations. The cask stores up to XX fuel assemblies.

    b. Description

    The XXXXXX Cask System is certified as described in the Safety Analysis Report (SAR) and in NRC's Safety Evaluation Report (SER) accompanying the Certificate of Compliance. The cask comprises three discrete components: the canister, the YYYYY transfer cask, and the XXXXX storage overpack.

NRC FORM 651A
(3-1999)
10 CFR 72

U.S. NUCLEAR REGULATORY COMMISSION

CERTIFICATE OF COMPLIANCE
FOR SPENT FUEL STORAGE CASKS
Supplemental Sheet

Certificate No.   XXXX

Page   2   of   4

1.   b.   Description (continued)

[The canister is the confinement system for the stored fuel. It is a welded, cylindrical container with a honeycombed fuel basket, a baseplate, a lid, a closure ring, and the canister shell. It is made entirely of stainless steel except for the neutron absorbers and aluminum heat conduction elements. The canister shell, baseplate, lid, vent and drain port cover plates, and closure ring are the main confinement boundary components. The honeycombed basket, which is equipped with Boral neutron absorbers, provides criticality control. The canister holds up to XX PWR fuel assemblies that must be intact.

The YYYY transfer cask provides shielding and structural protection of the canister during loading, unloading, and movement of the canister from the spent fuel pool to the storage overpack. The transfer cask is a multi-walled (carbon steel/lead/carbon steel) cylindrical vessel with a water jacket attached to the exterior. The maximum weight of a loaded transfer cask during any loading, unloading, or transfer operation is XXX tons.

The XXXX storage overpack provides shielding and structural protection of the canister during storage. The overpack is a heavy-walled, steel and concrete, cylindrical vessel. Its side wall consists of plain concrete that is enclosed between inner and outer carbon steel shells. The overpack has four air inlets at the bottom and four air outlets at the top to allow air to circulate naturally through the cavity to cool the canister inside. The inner shell has channels attached to its interior surface to guide the canister during insertion and removal, provide a flexible medium to absorb impact loads, and allow cooling air to circulate through the overpack. A loaded canister is stored within the XXXX storage overpack in a vertical orientation.]

2.   OPERATING PROCEDURES

Written operating procedures shall be prepared for cask handling, loading, unloading, movement, surveillance, and maintenance. The user's site-specific written operating procedures shall be consistent with the technical basis described in Chapter 8 of the SAR.

3.   ACCEPTANCE TESTS AND MAINTENANCE PROGRAM

Written cask acceptance tests and maintenance program shall be prepared consistent with the technical basis described in Chapter 9 of the SAR.

The heat transfer characteristics of the cask system will be recorded by temperature measurements for the first Spent Fuel Storage Canister (SFSC) System placed into service with a heat load equal to or greater than XX kW. An analysis shall be performed that demonstrates the temperature measurements validate the analytic methods and predicted thermal behavior described in Chapter 4 of the SAR.

Validation tests shall be performed for each subsequent cask system that has a heat load that exceeds a previously validated heat load by more than X kW. (e.g., if the initial test was conducted at XX kW, then no additional testing is needed until the heat load exceeds XX kW). No additional testing is required for a system after it has been tested at a heat load equal to or greater than XX kW.

Letter reports summarizing the results of each validation test shall be submitted to the NRC in accordance with 10 CFR 72.4. Cask users may satisfy these requirements by referencing validation test reports submitted to the NRC by other cask users.

4.   QUALITY ASSURANCE

Activities in the areas of design, purchase, fabrication, assembly, inspection, testing, operation, maintenance, repair, modification of structures, systems and components, and decommissioning that are important to safety shall be conducted in accordance with a Commission-approved quality assurance program which satisfies the applicable requirements of 10 CFR Part 72, Subpart G, and which is established, maintained, and executed with regard to the cask system.

5.   HEAVY LOADS REQUIREMENTS

Each lift of a canister, a YYYY transfer cask, or a XXXX overpack must be made in accordance with the existing heavy loads requirements and procedures of the licensed facility at which the lift is made. A plant-specific safety review (under 10 CFR 50.59 or 10 CFR 72.48, if applicable) is required to show operational compliance with existing plant-specific heavy loads requirements. Lifting operations outside of structures governed by 10 CFR Part 50 must be in accordance with Section 4.4 (Cask Transfer Operations) of the Appendix to this certificate.

6.   APPROVED CONTENTS

Contents of the XXXX Cask System must meet the fuel description as provided for in the Appendix to this certificate.

7.   DESIGN FEATURES

Features or characteristics for the site, cask, or ancillary equipment must be in accordance with the Appendix to this certificate.

NRC FORM 651A
(3-1999)
10 CFR 72

**CERTIFICATE OF COMPLIANCE
FOR SPENT FUEL STORAGE CASKS**
Supplemental Sheet

U.S. NUCLEAR REGULATORY COMMISSION

Certificate No.   XXXX

Page   4   of   4

8.   PRE-OPERATIONAL TESTING AND TRAINING EXERCISE

A dry run training exercise of the loading, closure, handling, unloading, and transfer of the Cask System shall be conducted by the licensee prior to the first use of the system to load spent fuel assemblies. The training exercise shall not be conducted with spent fuel in the canister. The dry run may be performed in an alternate step sequence from the actual procedures, but all steps must be performed. The dry run shall include, but is not limited to the following:

a. [Each applicant shall list the procedures important to its design.]

9.   CHANGES TO THE CERTIFICATE OF COMPLIANCE

The holder of this certificate who desires to make changes to the certificate, which includes the Appendix (Technical Specifications) shall submit an application for amendment of the certificate.

10.   AUTHORIZATION

The XXXX Cask System, which is authorized by this certificate, is hereby approved for general use by holders of 10 CFR Part 50 licenses for nuclear reactors at reactor sites under the general license issued pursuant to 10 CFR 72.210, subject to the conditions specified by 10 CFR 72.212, and the attached Appendix.

FOR THE U. S. NUCLEAR REGULATORY COMMISSION

E. William Brach, Director
Spent Fuel Project Office
Office of Nuclear Material Safety
and Safeguards

Attachment: Appendix to Certificate of Compliance No. XXXX

APPENDIX TO

CERTIFICATE OF COMPLIANCE No. XXXX

STANDARDIZED TECHNICAL SPECIFICATIONS

FOR THE NRC SAMPLE STORAGE CASK

TABLE OF CONTENTS

1.0 USE AND APPLICATION

1.1 Definitions

---NOTE---
The defined terms of this section appear in capitalized type and are applicable throughout these Technical Specifications and Bases. [Example definitions are given and changes or additional definitions such as DAMAGED FUEL or FUEL DEBRIS may be needed to be consistent with a particular design.]

Term	Definition
ACTIONS	ACTIONS shall be that part of a Specification that prescribes Required Actions to be taken under designated Conditions within specified Completion Times.
[CANISTER	The CANISTER is the sealed SPENT NUCLEAR FUEL container which consists of a basket contained in a cylindrical shell which is welded to a baseplate, lid with welded port cover plates, and closure ring. The CANISTER provides the confinement boundary for the contained radioactive materials.
INTACT FUEL ASSEMBLY	INTACT FUEL ASSEMBLY is a fuel assembly without known or suspected cladding defects greater than a pinhole leak or a hairline crack and which can be handled by normal means. A fuel assembly shall not be classified as an INTACT FUEL ASSEMBLY unless solid Zircaloy or stainless steel rods are used to replace missing fuel rods and which displace an amount of water equal to that displaced by the original fuel rod(s).
LOADING OPERATIONS	LOADING OPERATIONS include all licensed activities on an OVERPACK or TRANSFER CASK while it is being loaded with fuel assemblies. LOADING OPERATIONS begin when the first fuel assembly is placed in the CANISTER and end when the OVERPACK or TRANSFER CASK is suspended from or secured on the transporter. LOADING OPERATIONS does not include CANISTER transfer between the TRANSFER CASK and the OVERPACK.

(continued)

OPERABLE/OPERABILITY	A system, component, or device shall be OPERABLE or have OPERABILITY when it is capable of performing its specified safety function(s) and when all necessary attendant instrumentation, controls, normal or emergency electrical power, and other auxiliary equipment that are required for the system, component, or device to perform its specified safety function(s) are also capable of performing their related support function(s).
OVERPACK	OVERPACK is the cask which receives and contains the sealed CANISTER for interim storage in the independent spent fuel storage instillation (ISFSI). It provides gamma and neutron shielding, and provides for ventilated air flow to promote heat transfer from the CANISTER to the environs. The OVERPACK does not include the TRANSFER CASK.
SPENT FUEL STORAGE CASKS (SFSCs)	SFSCs are containers approved for the storage of spent fuel assemblies at the ISFSI. The [XXXX] SFSC System consists of the OVERPACK and its integral CANISTER.]
SPENT NUCLEAR FUEL	SPENT NUCLEAR FUEL means fuel that has been withdrawn from a nuclear reactor following irradiation, has undergone at least one year's decay since being used as a source of energy in a power reactor and has not been chemically separated into its constituent elements by reprocessing. SPENT NUCLEAR FUEL includes the special nuclear material, byproduct material, source material, and other radioactive materials associated with fuel assemblies.
[STORAGE OPERATIONS	STORAGE OPERATIONS include all licensed activities that are performed at the ISFSI while an SFSC containing spent fuel is sitting on a storage pad within the ISFSI perimeter. STORAGE OPERATIONS does not include CANISTER transfer between the TRANSFER CASK and the OVERPACK.
TRANSFER CASK	TRANSFER CASKs are containers designed to contain the CANISTER during and after loading of spent fuel assemblies and to transfer the CANISTER to or from the OVERPACK.

(continued)

1.1 Definitions (continued)

TRANSPORT OPERATIONSTRANSPORT OPERATIONS include all licensed activities performed on an OVERPACK or TRANSFER CASK loaded with one or more fuel assemblies when it is being moved to and from the ISFSI. TRANSPORT OPERATIONS begin when the OVERPACK or TRANSFER CASK is first suspended from or secured on the transporter and end when the OVERPACK or TRANSFER CASK is at its destination and no longer secured on or suspended from the transporter. TRANSPORT OPERATIONS include transfer of the CANISTER between the OVERPACK and the TRANSFER CASK.

UNLOADING OPERATIONS UNLOADING OPERATIONS include all licensed activities on an SFSC to be unloaded of the contained fuel assemblies. UNLOADING OPERATIONS begin when the OVERPACK or TRANSFER CASK is no longer suspended from or secured on the transporter and end when the last fuel assembly is removed from the SFSC. UNLOADING OPERATIONS do not include CANISTER transfer between the TRANSFER CASK and the OVERPACK.]

1.0 USE AND APPLICATION

<u>1.2 Logical Connectors</u>

PURPOSE
    The purpose of this section is to explain the meaning of logical connectors.

    Logical connectors are used in Technical Specifications (TS) to discriminate between, and yet connect, discrete Conditions, Required Actions, Completion Times, Surveillances, and Frequencies. The only logical connectors that appear in TS are <u>AND</u> and <u>OR</u>. The physical arrangement of these connectors constitutes logical conventions with specific meanings.

BACKGROUND
    Several levels of logic may be used to state Required Actions. These levels are identified by the placement (or nesting) of the logical connectors and by the number assigned to each Required Action. The first level of logic is identified by the first digit of the number assigned to a Required Action and the placement of the logical connector in the first level of nesting (i.e., left justified with the number of the Required Action). The successive levels of logic are identified by additional digits of the Required Action number and by successive indentions of the logical connectors.

    When logical connectors are used to state a Condition, Completion Time, Surveillance, or Frequency, only the first level of logic is used, and the logical connector is left justified with the statement of the Condition, Completion Time, Surveillance, or Frequency.

(continued)

EXAMPLES   The following examples illustrate the use of logical connectors.

EXAMPLE 1.2-1

ACTIONS

CONDITION	REQUIRED ACTION	COMPLETION TIME
A. LCO not met.	A.1 Verify . . . AND A.2 Restore . . .	

In this example, the logical connector AND is used to indicate that when in Condition A, both Required Actions A.1 and A.2 must be completed.

(continued)

1.2 Logical Connectors (continued)

EXAMPLES
(continued)

EXAMPLE 1.2-2

ACTIONS

CONDITION	REQUIRED ACTION	COMPLETION TIME
A.　　LCO not met.	A.1　　Stop . . . OR A.2.1　Verify . . . 　　　AND A.2.2.1 Reduce . . . 　　　　OR A.2.2.2 Perform . . . OR A.3　　Remove. . .	

This example represents a more complicated use of logical connectors. Required Actions A.1, A.2, and A.3 are alternative choices, only one of which must be performed as indicated by the use of the logical connector OR and the left justified placement. Any one of these three ACTIONS may be chosen. If A.2 is chosen, then both A.2.1 and A.2.2 must be performed as indicated by the logical connector AND. Required Action A.2.2 is met by performing A.2.2.1 or A.2.2.2. The indented position of the logical connector OR indicates that A.2.2.1 and A.2.2.2 are alternative choices, only one of which must be performed.

1.0 USE AND APPLICATION

1.3 Completion Times

PURPOSE	The purpose of this section is to establish the Completion Time convention and to provide guidance for its use.

BACKGROUND	Limiting Conditions for Operation (LCOs) specify the lowest functional capability or performance levels of equipment required for safe operation of the facility. The ACTIONS associated with an LCO state Conditions that typically describe the ways in which the requirements of the LCO can fail to be met. Specified with each stated Condition are Required Action(s) and Completion Times(s).

DESCRIPTION	The Completion Time is the amount of time allowed for completing a Required Action. It is referenced to the time of discovery of a situation (e.g., equipment or variable not within limits) that requires entering an ACTIONS Condition unless otherwise specified, providing the Cask System is in a specified condition stated in the Applicability of the LCO. Required Actions must be completed prior to the expiration of the specified Completion Time. An ACTIONS Condition remains in effect and the Required Actions apply until the Condition no longer exists or the Cask System is not within the LCO Applicability.

Once a Condition has been entered, subsequent subsystems, components, or variables expressed in the Condition, discovered to be not within limits, will not result in separate entry into the Condition unless specifically stated. The Required Actions of the Condition continue to apply to each additional failure, with Completion Times based on initial entry into the Condition. |

(continued)

1.3 Completion Times (continued)

EXAMPLES   The following examples illustrate the use of Completion Times with
                  different types of Conditions and changing Conditions.

                  EXAMPLE 1.3-1

                  ACTIONS

CONDITION	REQUIRED ACTION	COMPLETION TIME
B. Required Action and associated Completion Time not met.	B.1 Perform Action B.1. AND B.2 Perform Action B.2.	12 hours 36 hours

Condition B has two Required Actions. Each Required Action has its own
separate Completion Time. Each Completion Time is referenced to the
time that Condition B is entered.

The Required Actions of Condition B are to complete action B.1 within 12
hours AND complete action B.2 within 36 hours. A total of 12 hours is
allowed for completing action B.1 and a total of 36 hours (not 48 hours) is
allowed for completing action B.2 from the time that Condition B was
entered. If action B.1 is completed within 6 hours, the time allowed for
completing action B.2 is the next 30 hours because the total time allowed
for completing action B.2 is 36 hours.

(continued)

1.3 Completion Times (continued)

EXAMPLES
(continued)

EXAMPLE 1.3-2

ACTIONS

CONDITION	REQUIRED ACTION		COMPLETION TIME
A. One system not within limit.	A.1	Restore system to within limit.	7 days
B. Required Action and associated Completion Time not met.	B.1	Complete action B.1.	12 hours
	AND		
	B.2	Complete action B.2.	36 hours

When a system is determined not to meet the LCO, Condition A is entered. If the system is not restored within 7 days, Condition B is also entered and the Completion Time clocks for Required Actions B.1 and B.2 start. If the system is restored after Condition B is entered, Conditions A and B are exited, and therefore, the Required Actions of Condition B may be terminated.

(continued)

1.3 Completion Times (continued)

EXAMPLES
(continued)

EXAMPLE 1.3-3

ACTIONS

------------------------------------NOTE------------------------------------
Separate Condition entry is allowed for each component.

CONDITION	REQUIRED ACTION	COMPLETION TIME
A. LCO not met.	A.1 Restore compliance with LCO.	4 hours
B. Required Action and associated Completion Time not met.	B.1 Complete action B.1. AND B.2 Complete action B.2.	6 hours 12 hours

The Note above the ACTIONS table is a method of modifying how the Completion Time is tracked. If this method of modifying how the Completion Time is tracked was applicable only to a specific Condition, the Note would appear in that Condition rather than at the top of the ACTIONS Table.

The Note allows Condition A to be entered separately for each component and Completion Times tracked on a per component basis. When a component is determined to not meet the LCO, Condition A is entered and its Completion Time starts. If subsequent components are determined to not meet the LCO, Condition A is entered for each component and separate Completion Times start and are tracked for each component.

IMMEDIATE
COMPLETION
TIME

When "Immediately" is used as a Completion Time, the Required Action should be pursued without delay and in a controlled manner.

1.0 USE AND APPLICATION

1.4 Frequency

PURPOSE
The purpose of this section is to define the proper use and application of Frequency requirements.

DESCRIPTION
Each Surveillance Requirement (SR) has a specified Frequency in which the Surveillance must be met in order to meet the associated Limiting Condition for Operation (LCO). An understanding of the correct application of the specified Frequency is necessary for compliance with the SR.

The "specified Frequency" is referred to throughout this section and each of the Specifications of Section 3.0, Surveillance Requirement (SR) Applicability. The "specified Frequency" consists of the requirements of the Frequency column of each SR.

Situations where a Surveillance could be required (i.e., its Frequency could expire), but where it is not possible or not desired that it be performed until sometime after the associated LCO is within its Applicability, represent potential SR 3.0.4 conflicts. To avoid these conflicts, the SR (i.e., the Surveillance or the Frequency) is stated such that it is only "required" when it can be and should be performed. With an SR satisfied, SR 3.0.4 imposes no restriction.

(continued)

1.4 Frequency (continued)

EXAMPLES   The following examples illustrate the various ways that Frequencies are
                  specified.

                  EXAMPLE 1.4-1

                  SURVEILLANCE REQUIREMENTS

SURVEILLANCE	FREQUENCY
Verify pressure within limit.	12 hours

                  Example 1.4-1 contains the type of SR most often encountered in the
                  Technical Specifications (TS). The Frequency specifies an interval
                  (12 hours) during which the associated Surveillance must be performed
                  at least one time. Performance of the Surveillance initiates the
                  subsequent interval. Although the Frequency is stated as 12 hours, an
                  extension of the time interval to 1.25 times the interval specified in the
                  Frequency is allowed by SR 3.0.2 for operational flexibility. The
                  measurement of this interval continues at all times, even when the SR is
                  not required to be met per SR 3.0.1 (such as when the equipment or
                  variables are outside specified limits, or the facility is outside the
                  Applicability of the LCO). If the interval specified by SR 3.0.2 is exceeded
                  while the facility is in a condition specified in the Applicability of the LCO,
                  the LCO is not met in accordance with SR 3.0.1.

                  If the interval as specified by SR 3.0.2 is exceeded while the facility is not
                  in a condition specified in the Applicability of the LCO for which
                  performance of the SR is required, the Surveillance must be performed
                  within the Frequency requirements of SR 3.0.2 prior to entry into the
                  specified condition. Failure to do so would result in a violation of SR
                  3.0.4

(continued)

1.4 Frequency (continued)

EXAMPLES
(continued)   EXAMPLE 1.4-2

SURVEILLANCE REQUIREMENTS

SURVEILLANCE	FREQUENCY
Verify flow is within limits.	Once within 12 hours prior to starting activity AND 24 hours thereafter

Example 1.4-2 has two Frequencies. The first is a one time performance Frequency, and the second is of the type shown in Example 1.4-1. The logical connector "AND" indicates that both Frequency requirements must be met. Each time the example activity is to be performed, the Surveillance must be performed within 12 hours prior to starting the activity.

The use of "once" indicates a single performance will satisfy the specified Frequency (assuming no other Frequencies are connected by "AND"). This type of Frequency does not qualify for the 25% extension allowed by SR 3.0.2.

"Thereafter" indicates future performances must be established per SR 3.0.2, but only after a specified condition is first met (i.e., the "once" performance in this example). If the specified activity is canceled or not performed, the measurement of both intervals stops. New intervals start upon preparing to restart the specified activity.

2.0   APPROVED CONTENTS

2.1   Cask contents shall be limited to SPENT NUCLEAR FUEL initially approved by the NRC in Appendix [X.XX] of the FSAR, through the issuance of a cask Certificate of Compliance.

2.2   Proposed alternatives to contents listed in Appendix [X.XX] of the FSAR may be authorized by the Director of The Office of Nuclear Material Safety and Safeguards or designee. The request for such alternative contents should demonstrate that:

1.   The proposed alternative contents would provide an acceptable level of safety, and

2.   The proposed alternative contents are consistent with the applicable requirements.

Requests for alternatives to contents shall be submitted in accordance with 10 CFR 72.4.

[A description of the fuel parameters to be listed in Appendix [X.XX] is provided below:
    Fissile Isotopes (UO_2 vs. MOX)
    Maximum Initial [Planar Average] Enrichment
    Fuel Class (e.g., 14x14, 15x15)
        Number of Fuel Rods
        Number of Water Holes
    Maximum Assembly Average Burnup
    Minimum Cooling Time after Reactor Shutdown
    Minimum Active Fuel Average Enrichment
    Cladding Material
    Non-Fuel Hardware (e.g., BPRA/TPAs (cooling time and burnup))
    Maximum Weight per Storage Location (including fuel channels and non-fuel hardware)
    Maximum Decay Heat per Storage Location
    Fuel Condition (intact, damaged or debris)

To change these parameters requires NRC approval. All other fuel parameters, also identified in the FSAR, can be changed through the 10 CFR 72.48 process. The parameter list may need to be modified based on unique features of a particular design or for specialized areas such as high burnup fuel and burnup credit. This list is intended for intact fuel. As a result, the list may need to be modified if damaged fuel or fuel debris is stored in the cask.

When preferential loading configurations are part of the design basis, they need to be included in the contents description.]

3.0 LIMITING CONDITION FOR OPERATION (LCO) APPLICABILITY

LCO 3.0.1 LCOs shall be met during specified conditions in the Applicability, except as provided in LCO 3.0.2.

LCO 3.0.2 Upon discovery of a failure to meet an LCO, the Required Actions of the associated Conditions shall be met.

If the LCO is met or is no longer applicable prior to expiration of the specified Completion Time(s), completion of the Required Action(s) is not required, unless otherwise stated.

LCO 3.0.3 Not applicable.

LCO 3.0.4 When an LCO is not met, entry into a specified condition in the Applicability shall not be made except when the associated ACTIONS to be entered permit continued operation in the specified condition in the Applicability for an unlimited period of time. This Specification shall not prevent changes in specified conditions in the Applicability that are required to comply with ACTIONS or that are related to the unloading of an SFSC.

LCO 3.0.5 Not applicable.

3.0 SURVEILLANCE REQUIREMENT (SR) APPLICABILITY

SR 3.0.1   SRs shall be met during the specified conditions in the Applicability for individual LCOs, unless otherwise stated in the SR. Failure to meet a Surveillance, whether such failure is experienced during the performance of the Surveillance or between performances of the Surveillance, shall be failure to meet the LCO. Failure to perform a Surveillance within the specified Frequency shall be failure to meet the LCO except as provided in SR 3.0.3. Surveillances do not have to be performed on equipment or variables outside specified limits.

SR 3.0.2   The specified Frequency for each SR is met if the Surveillance is performed within 1.25 times the interval specified in the Frequency, as measured from the previous performance or as measured from the time a specified condition of the Frequency is met.

For Frequencies specified as "once," the above interval extension does not apply. If a Completion Time requires periodic performance on a "once per..." basis, the above Frequency extension applies to each performance after the initial performance.

Exceptions to this Specification are stated in the individual Specifications.

SR 3.0.3   If it is discovered that a Surveillance was not performed within its specified Frequency, then compliance with the requirement to declare the LCO not met may be delayed, from the time of discovery, up to 24 hours or up to the limit of the specified Frequency, whichever is less. This delay period is permitted to allow performance of the Surveillance.

If the Surveillance is not performed within the delay period, the LCO must immediately be declared not met, and the applicable Condition(s) must be entered. When the Surveillance is performed within the delay period and the Surveillance is not met, the LCO must immediately be declared not met, and the applicable Condition(s) must be entered.

SR 3.0.4   Entry into a specified condition in the Applicability of an LCO shall not be made unless the LCO's Surveillances have been met within their specified Frequency. This provision shall not prevent entry into specified conditions in the Applicability that are required to comply with Actions or that are related to the unloading of an SFSC.

3.1 Fuel Integrity

3.1.1 Fuel Integrity During Drying

LCO 3.1.1 The time after draining the [CANISTER/Cask] and before helium backfill operation is complete shall not exceed [X] days [the vacuum drying time may be a function of decay heat in a table or chart].

[NOTE: The time specification [X] may be relocated to an administrative program if a methodology for calculating fuel temperature based on decay heat and heatup time is approved by the NRC.]

APPLICABILITY: During LOADING OPERATIONS.

ACTIONS:
---NOTE---
Separate Condition entry is allowed for each [CANISTER/Cask].

CONDITION		REQUIRED ACTION	COMPLETION TIME
A.	LCO not met.	A.1 Verify adequate heat removal to prevent exceeding a short-term fuel temperature limit.	Immediately
		AND	
		A.2 Complete helium backfill operation.	[X] days
B.	Required Actions and associated Completion Times not met.	B.1 Place [CANISTER/Cask] in [a safe condition. The applicant shall propose an appropriate condition and completion time for its design.]	Immediately

(continued)

SURVEILLANCE REQUIREMENTS

	SURVEILLANCE	FREQUENCY
SR 3.1.1	Verify the time after draining the [CANISTER/Cask] and before helium backfill operation is completed is $\leq$ [X] days. SR 3.0.4 does not apply.	Once, prior to TRANSPORT operations

3.1 Fuel Integrity
_____

3.1.2 Fuel Integrity During Backfill and Transfer

LCO 3.1.2   The time after completion of helium backfill operation and until the
                   CANISTER is inserted into the storage cask shall not exceed [X] days [the
                   time may be a function of decay heat in a table or chart].

*[NOTE: This LCO may not be needed if the associated casks and approved contents provide
adequate cooling to prevent approaching short–term fuel temperature limits. The time
specification [X] may be relocated to an administrative program if a methodology for calculating
fuel temperature based on decay heat and heatup time is approved by the NRC. A similar type
LCO may be needed for UNLOADING operations.]*

APPLICABILITY: During LOADING OPERATIONS.

ACTIONS:
---NOTE--
Separate Condition entry is allowed for each CANISTER.

CONDITION	REQUIRED ACTION	COMPLETION TIME
A. LCO not met.	A.1 Verify adequate heat removal to prevent exceeding a short-term fuel temperature limit.	Immediately
	AND	
	A.2 Complete CANISTER transfer.	[X] days
B. Required Actions and associated Completion Times not met.	B.1 Place CANISTER in [a safe condition. The applicant shall propose an appropriate condition and completion·time for its design.]	Immediately

(continued)

	SURVEILLANCE	FREQUENCY
SR 3.1.2	Verify that the time after completion of helium backfill operation and until insertion of the CANISTER into the storage cask is ≤ [X] days. SR 3.0.4 does not apply.	Once, prior to TRANSPORT operations

Note: this LCO is only applicable to cask designs with cooling vents.

3.1 Fuel Integrity

3.1.3 SFSC Heat Removal System

LCO 3.1.3 The SFSC Heat Removal System shall be OPERABLE

APPLICABILITY: While CANISTER is in the storage OVERPACK.

ACTIONS:
---NOTE--
Separate Condition entry is allowed for each SFSC.

CONDITION	REQUIRED ACTION	COMPLETION TIME
A. LCO not met.	A.1 Restore SFSC Heat Removal System to OPERABLE status. OR A.2.1 Verify adequate heat removal to prevent exceeding short-term fuel temperature limit; AND A.2.2 Restore SFSC Heat Removal System to OPERABLE status.	[8] hours Immediately [30] days
B. Required Actions and associated Completion Times not met.	B.1 Place SFSC in [a safe condition. The applicant shall propose an appropriate condition and completion time for its design.]	Immediately

(continued)

SURVEILLANCE REQUIREMENTS

	SURVEILLANCE	FREQUENCY
SR 3.1.3	Verify all OVERPACK inlet and outlet air ducts are free of blockage.	[24] hours
	OR	
	For OVERPACKS with temperature monitoring equipment, verify the difference between the average OVERPACK air outlet temperature and ISFSI ambient temperature is [≤ XX° F or C].	[24] hours

Note: Required only for those casks with bolted closures and an interseal pressure monitoring system.

3.2 Cask Integrity

3.2.1 Cask Interseal Pressure

LCO 3.2.1   The cask interseal minimum pressure shall be maintained at the value listed in Section xxxx of the FSAR, as updated.

APPLICABILITY: During STORAGE OPERATIONS.

ACTION:

--NOTE--
Separate Condition entry is allowed for each SFSC.

CONDITION	REQUIRED ACTION	COMPLETION TIME
A. Cask interseal pressure below limit.	A.1 Re-establish cask interseal pressure above limit.	[7] days
B. Required Action and associated Completion time not met.	B.1 Place SFSC in [a safe condition. The applicant shall propose an appropriate condition and completion time for its design.]	[30] days

(continued)

SURVEILLANCE REQUIREMENTS

	SURVEILLANCE	FREQUENCY
SR 3.2.1	Verify cask interseal helium pressure above limit.	[7] days
SR 3.2.2	Perform a channel operational test to verify proper function of pressure switch/transducer on cask overpressure system.	Once, within [7] days of commencing storage operations and every [36] months thereafter

Note: Required only for those casks that take credit for boron in the water for criticality control. Not needed for BWR plants.

3.3 Cask Criticality Control Program

3.3.1 Dissolved Boron Concentration

LCO 3.3.1   The dissolved boron concentration in the water of the [CANISTER/Cask] cavity shall be $\geq$ [XXX] ppmb.

[NOTE: The boron concentration [XXX] may be relocated to an administrative program if a methodology for calculating k-eff of the spent fuel storage [CANISTER/Cask] is approved by the NRC.]

APPLICABILITY: During LOADING OPERATIONS and UNLOADING OPERATIONS with water and at least one fuel assembly in the [CANISTER/Cask]

ACTIONS:

CONDITION	REQUIRED ACTION	COMPLETION TIME
A. Dissolved boron concentration not met.	A.1 Suspend loading of fuel assemblies into cask and any other actions that increase reactivity.	Immediately
	AND	
	A.2 Restore boron concentration to exceed limit.	Immediately
	AND	
	A.3 Remove all fuel assemblies from cask.	[24] hours

(continued)

SURVEILLANCE REQUIREMENTS

SURVEILLANCE		FREQUENCY
SR 3.3.1.1	Verify the dissolved boron concentration is met using two independent measurements.	Within [4] hours prior to commencing LOADING OPERATIONS AND every [48] hours thereafter while the cask is in the spent fuel pool or while water is in the cask
SR 3.3.1.2	Verify the dissolved boron concentration is met using two independent measurements.	Within [4] hours prior to commencing UNLOADING OPERATIONS AND every [48] hours thereafter while the cask is in the spent fuel pool or while water is in the cask

Note: This specification is only required if:
a. Boron credit is assumed in the criticality analysis, and/or
b. Optimum moderation is not assumed in the criticality analysis.

3.3.2   [CANISTER/Cask] Water Temperature

LCO 3.3.2   The temperature of the water in the canister shall be ≤ 200 °F [alternatively, in lieu of a temperature limit, a time limit can be applied that is based on decay heat].

APPLICABILITY: During LOADING and UNLOADING OPERATIONS.

ACTIONS:

---NOTE---
Separate Condition entry is allowed for each [CANISTER/Cask] system.

CONDITION	REQUIRED ACTION	COMPLETION TIME
A. [CANISTER/Cask] water temperature limit not met.	A.1 Restore [CANISTER/Cask] water temperature to below limit.	[2] hours
B. Required Action and Associated Completion time not met.	B.1 Place [CANISTER/Cask] in [a safe condition. The applicant shall propose an appropriate condition and completion time for its design.]	Immediately

(continued)

SURVEILLANCE REQUIREMENTS

	SURVEILLANCE	FREQUENCY
SR 3.3.2	Verify temperature of the water in the [CANISTER/Cask] has not exceeded 200 °F.	Once within [18] hours after [TRANSFER CASK with loaded CANISTER/Cask] is removed from fuel pool AND Every [30] minutes thereafter

4.0 DESIGN FEATURES

4.1 Design Features Significant to Safety

4.1.1 Criticality Control

[Items listed in 4.1.1 are those which would have a significant effect on safety if altered or modified. Item 1 and/or 2 may be removed if the application includes an analysis which shows that the parameter does not significantly affect criticality safety in the particular design.]

1. Flux trap size or fuel cell spacing: $\geq$ [X.XX] in.
2. ^{10}B loading in the Boral neutron absorbers: $\geq$ [X.XX] g/cm^2

[4.1.2 Materials

1. Protective coatings used inside the cask
2. Neutron Absorbers and Shields
3. Containment Boundary Seals

Instead of specifying a material directly, the applicant may propose a set of performance standards along with proposed methods for determining that the material will meet the applicable standards.

Note: Section 4.1.2 may be incorporated into the Cask Description in Condition 1.b. of the Certificate of Compliance if the applicant prefers.]

4.2 Codes and Standards

The following provides information on the governing codes for components of the [XXX] cask design:

Cask Component Important to Safety	Applicable Codes	Editions/Years
[XXXX]	[XXXXXX]	[XXXXX]

4.2.1 Alternatives to Codes, Standards, and Criteria

Table [X.XX] of the FSAR lists approved alternatives to the [code(s) of record] for the design of the Cask System.

(continued)

4.2.2 Construction/Fabrication Alternatives to Codes, Standards, and Criteria

Proposed alternatives to the [code(s) of record] including alternatives allowed by Table X.XX of the FSAR may be used when authorized by the Director of the Office of Nuclear Material Safety and Safeguards or designee. The request for such alternatives should demonstrate that:

1. The proposed alternatives would provide an acceptable level of quality and safety, or

2. Compliance with the specified requirements of the [code of record] would result in hardship or unusual difficulty without a compensating increase in the level of quality and safety.

Requests for alternatives shall be submitted in accordance with 10 CFR 72.4.

4.3 Structural Performance

4.3.1 Earthquake Loads

The spent fuel storage cask design earthquake load on the top surface of the ISFSI pad shall not exceed:

Horizontal Peak Acceleration in each of the two orthogonal Directions	Corresponding Vertical Peak Accelerations
[XX]	[XX]

4.3.2 Design G-loads

The fission product barrier design g-loads due to postulated handling accidents shall not exceed:

Fission Product Barrier	End Drop	Side Drop	Tipover
[Cask and/or CANISTER]	[XX]	[XX]	[XX]

4.4 Cask Handling/ CANISTER Transfer Facility
[Note that certain designs may require a specification for operations outside of the Part 50 facility.]

5.0 ADMINISTRATIVE CONTROLS

5.1 Administrative Programs

The following programs shall be established, implemented, and maintained:

5.1.1 Radioactive Effluent Control Program

A program shall be established that includes:

1. Implementation of the requirements of [10 CFR 72.44(d) or 72.126, as appropriate].
2. Limits on the surface contamination and verification of meeting those limits prior to removal of the cask from the Part 50 structure,
3. Limits on the leakage rate and verification of meeting those limits prior to removal of the cask from the Part 50 structure, and,
4. An effluent monitoring program, if the surface contamination limits are greater than the values specified in [Regulatory Guide 1.86 or an NRC-approved methodology in the FSAR can be inserted in place of RG-1.86]; or if the leakage rate limits are greater than the values specified as "leaktight" in [ANSI N14.5 - 1997 "Leakage Tests on Packages for Shipment" or an NRC-approved methodology in the FSAR can be inserted in place of ANSI N14.5].

5.1.2 Cask Loading, Unloading, and Preparation Program

A program shall be established to implement the FSAR requirements for loading fuel and components into the cask, unloading fuel and components from the cask, and preparing the cask for storage. The requirements of the program for loading and preparing the cask shall be complete prior to removing the cask from the 10 CFR Part 50 structure. [Items 1, 5, and 6 are associated with requirements that will remain in the STS, however, the process for establishing the specified action limit may be moved to this administrative program if a method of evaluation acceptable to the NRC is presented in the FSAR. Items 2, 3, and 4 have been relocated from the LCO section to this administrative program because it is felt that NRC approved methods of evaluation will be relatively easy to develop. If appropriate methods are not presented in the FSAR, these items will retain LCOs.]

At a minimum, the program shall establish criteria that need to be verified to address FSAR commitments and regulatory requirements for:

1. Vacuum drying times and pressures to assure that the short-term fuel temperature limits are not violated and the cask is adequately dry,
2. Inerting pressure and purity to assure adequate heat transfer and corrosion control,
3. Leak testing to assure adequate cask integrity and consistency with the offsite dose analysis,

(continued)

4. Surface dose rates to assure proper loading and consistency with the offsite dose analysis,
5. Ambient and pool water temperature to assure adequate subcriticality and material ductility,
6. Spent fuel pool boron concentration to verify the acceptable subcriticality margin, and
7. [Clad oxidation thickness for high-burnup fuel in accordance with ISG-11 or other NRC-approved methodology if high-burnup fuel is included in the contents.]

The program shall include compensatory measures and appropriate completion times if the program requirements are not met.

5.1.3 ISFSI Operations Program

A program shall be established to implement the FSAR requirements for ISFSI Operations.

At a minimum, the program shall establish criteria that need to be verified for:

1. Minimum cask center-to-center spacing,
2. Pad parameters (i.e., pad thickness, concrete strength, soil modulus, reinforcement, etc.) that are consistent with the FSAR analysis, and
3. Maximum lifting heights for the cask system to ensure that the g-load limits in the table in Section 4.3.2 are met for the design basis events.

NRC FORM 335	U.S. NUCLEAR REGULATORY COMMISSION	1. REPORT NUMBER (Assigned by NRC, Add Vol., Supp., Rev., and Addendum Numbers, If any.)
(2-89) NRCM 1102, 3201, 3202	**BIBLIOGRAPHIC DATA SHEET** *(See instructions on the reverse)*	NUREG-1745

2. TITLE AND SUBTITLE		
Standard Format and Content for Technical Specifications for 10 CFR Part 72 Cask Certificates of Compliance	3. DATE REPORT PUBLISHED	
	MONTH: June	YEAR: 2001
	4. FIN OR GRANT NUMBER	

5. AUTHOR(S)	6. TYPE OF REPORT
C. Withee, C. Jackson, et al.	Technical
	7. PERIOD COVERED *(Inclusive Dates)*

8. PERFORMING ORGANIZATION - NAME AND ADDRESS *(If NRC, provide Division, Office or Region, U.S. Nuclear Regulatory Commission, and mailing address; if contractor, provide name and mailing address.)*

Spent Fuel Project Office
Office of Nuclear Material Safety and Safeguards
U.S. Nuclear Regulatory Commission
Washington, DC 20555-0001

9. SPONSORING ORGANIZATION - NAME AND ADDRESS *(If NRC, type "Same as above"; if contractor, provide NRC Division, Office or Region, U.S. Nuclear Regulatory Commission, and mailing address.)*

Same as 8. above.

10. SUPPLEMENTARY NOTES

11. ABSTRACT *(200 words or less)*

The Standard Technical Specifications (STS) for dry cask storage are intended to be used by potential 10 CFR Part 72 Certificate Holders in developing a set of clear and consistent technical specifications for their dry cask storage applications.

The NRC believes that these Dry Cask STS in this NUREG will assure the overall safety goals for dry case storage are met, including maintaining subcriticality, controlling radiation dose to the workers and the public, assuring fuel retrievability, and maintaining the confinement barriers. This effort has removed the unnecessary detail from the technical specifications, moved the less significant requirements to administrative programs, made the requirements less prescriptive and maintained consistency with the site specific requirements contained in 10 CFR 72.44. Although these STS were developed for Certificate Holders, the format and level of detail presented in this set of STS can easily be translated to technical specifications for site-specific licensees.

12. KEY WORDS/DESCRIPTORS *(List words or phrases that will assist researchers in locating the report.)*	13. AVAILABILITY STATEMENT
Spent Fuel Storage Cask Independent Spent Fuel Sorage Installation Standard Technical Specification	unlimited
	14. SECURITY CLASSIFICATION
	(This Page) unclassified
	(This Report) unclassified
	15. NUMBER OF PAGES
	16. PRICE

NRC FORM 335 (2-89)

Printed
on recycled
paper

Federal Recycling Program

NUREG-1745   STANDARD FORMAT AND CONTENT FOR TECHNICAL SPECIFICATIONS FOR 10 CFR PART 72   JUNE 2001
CERTIFICATES OF COMPLIANCE

UNITED STATES
NUCLEAR REGULATORY COMMISSION
WASHINGTON, DC 20555-0001

OFFICIAL BUSINESS
PENALTY FOR PRIVATE USE, $300